A JOURNEY TO
GENEROSITY

41 Days to a Generous Life

Michael L. Stickler

A Journey to Generosity
41 Days to a Generous Life
by MICHAEL L. STICKLER

Printed in the United States of America

ISBN 978-0-9907441-0-8

thevisiongroupltd.com

TABLE OF CONTENTS

INTRODUCTION

What is a **Generous Life?**

A Generous Life celebrates generosity lived in the name of Christ.

From the everyday kindnesses that help make someone's bad day livable to the extraordinary giving and care that changes lives forever, this little book seeks to enable everyone, from philanthropists to everyday people, to live the way God desires.

I want to take you on a 41-day journey. This journey will change your life, the lives of your family, your church, and your community.

Spend the next 41 days with me and with like travelers all around the world, as we begin to make a difference in others' lives.

Each day of your journey...

- Begin your day in prayer,
- As you read the day's entry, allow it to inspire you,
- Then, with boldness, attempt the daily challenge,
- Watch how others react,
- Make note of your own personal reaction to each challenge,
- Finally, return to GenerousLife.net, as explained in each daily challenge, and
- Journal your experiences.

When you journal, you'll be encouraging others to grow into

God's generous life along with you.

You can post stories of everyday generosity that you experience over the next 41 days – and beyond – the kind of stories you can use to inspire and inform your growing generosity and generosity in the lives of others.

As you travel this journey, you will see a pattern emerge in and around you that reflects God's extravagant generosity to you.

I pray that the next 41 days change you deeply.

Be bold, be encouraged, be generous.

Michael L. Stickler

ACKNOWLEDGEMENTS
- and -
Special Thanks to...

Jason Ching, editor and man-of-God whose tireless efforts and integrity honors the Lord.

Pastors Tony Slavin and Jay Hull, who have demonstrated time and time again thy have my back through thick and thin.

Pastor Pat Propster, whose life is a cold drink of water on a hot desert day. And always right when I needed refreshing.

My mentors, who were so powerfully used by God in my life: Art Barkley, Paul Sitze, and Chuck Colson.

And finally,

This book is dedicated to my wife Kim, the bride of my youth, my inspiration of Christ's generosity in service to the lives of others.

In His loving service....

Michael Stickler

FOREWORD
by Dr Tom Clegg

Have you noticed that every time you watch one of those TV programs where they give someone a lot of money, the break they've never gotten, or a house they could have never gotten on their own, like it or not, something happens inside of us? ... a lump in the throat? ... a catch in our voice? ... a tear in our eye? Every single time! Why is that? It happens because there is something in the heart of every one of us that knows and understands that being generous is connected to something profoundly unique to the human experience. Instinctively, we know that we know (down deep in our 'knower'), that being generous is right, good, sweet, and amazing. We want that kind of generosity to be in our lives.

So why aren't we?

Early on we were all taught to share; but, then, something happened as we grew. Sharing became less and less instinctive and more and more difficult. Being generous became the exception rather than the rule. Try as we might, being generous just doesn't come naturally anymore. So what can we do about that? Can a person learn to become more generous once again?

The answer is, **yes**.

The main reason we are not generous with who we are and what we have isn't really one of stinginess or greed. It is almost always because of fear. It's the fear that comes from trusting all the wrong things, pinning our hopes on things way too flimsy to bear the weight of our soul. Fear that we are on this journey all by ourselves.

So how can we overcome that fear?

What you hold in your hands is a powerful pathway out of those fears and into a better way of living. It's a pathway through the jungles of consumerism, scarcity, dissatisfaction, loneliness, and shame – to the place of growing contentment, connection, compassion and confidence. In other words, to that place we all want to be in life: Healthy. Balanced. Generous toward others. And most of all, unafraid.

In this practical and personal book, A Journey To Generosity, my friend and author, Mike Stickler walks with you on the first steps of your lifelong journey from fear to generosity. With a wisdom that can be forged only in the crucible of experience and a compassion that can be found only amidst severe testing, come 41 days of lessons, 41 opportunities to grow, 41 challenging questions, 41 thought-provoking stories, 41 gentle and not so gentle nudges that will empower you to face your fears daily and grow into a new season of growing generosity and Christlikeness.

Start your journey today...you'll be glad you did!

Tom Clegg

Dr. Clegg is the author of *Missing In America, Lost in America, Releasing Your Church's Potential, The Seven Habits of a Visitor-Friendly Church,* and *Mission America.*

Endorsements

"In his concise and potent guide to a generous life, Mike Stickler offers a very practical and biblically faithful tour of the fundamental principles of a life that invests in eternity by transmuting the lead of what is passing away into the gold of what will endure forever."
Dr. Kenneth Boa
KenBoa.org

"This devotional has challenged me in a most refreshing way on my journey of learning to be "generous on every occasion". These daily readings are fantastic reminders to rely on the truth in God's Word and to be led by His Spirit in generous living!"
Mike Weaver
Big Daddy Weave, Christian recording artist

"This book tells you step by step how to find the joy, responsibility, challenges and rewards God has for giving generously. You will find it also gives you a happy heart when you think about giving!"
Arch Bonnema
Philanthropist

"The church in America needs many things. A generous spirit and life is near the top of the list. Read this book and accept the challenge!"
Dr. John Jackson, President of William Jessup University
Author of six books on Transformational Leadership and Personal Renewal.

"The word "generous" originally had the meaning of a person from "noble birth." What it meant was that generous people were a cut above the crowd and because of their charity it seemed that they were from nobility. Mike has written a phenomenal book of what it means to walk in that nobility. If you want to change your life and change the lives of others you need to get this book, read it, re-read it, live it, and teach it. And then watch as you change the world one day at a time."

    Mike Holmes
    Tithehacker.com

"Discipling generous givers is one of the most pressing issues facing the church. Credible giving stats confirm that we need to recalibrate and evaluate what we've done and how to disciple generous givers more effectively. Mike's 'A Journey to Generosity – 41 Days to a Generous Life' is a resource that, if taken seriously, can help do that. One can quickly read the Scriptures, devotional and daily challenge and take steps towards becoming generous as Christ is generous."

    Chris McDaniel
    Author, *Igniting a Life of Generosity*
    Chief Business Development Officer for DELTA Ministries International

Day 1 - God is the Owner of everything

Psalm 50: 10-12
[10] for every animal of the forest is mine,
and the cattle on a thousand hills.
[11] I know every bird in the mountains,
and the creatures of the field are mine.
[12] If I were hungry I would not tell you,
for the world is mine, and all that is in it.

Psalm 50 tells us of the reality that we often do not acknowledge. The Lord describes that literally everything belongs to Him. In this psalm, the Lord uses the imagery of all the animals of the forest and all the cattle of a thousand hills. If it helps a modern listener, He could also have said that every skyscraper, bank, car, and computer is His, too. Using language that the everyday person can understand, He says that if He were ever hungry, He would have no reason to tell a man, because He owns everything in the world and He already has all that He needs. "The world is mine," the Lord says, "and all that is in it." The Lord makes no exceptions; He doesn't just own all the things that relate to the agriculture industry. Everything you have rightfully belongs to Him. Your money, your home, your car, the clothes on your back – even your very life. God created it all and He has the only rightful claim to it all.

How does this affect our daily lives? One thing that prevents Christians from being generous is that they have a hard time parting with the things they possess. But, if we take this psalm to heart, we realize that everything we have actually belongs to God. It always has and it always will. And if God tells us to be generous with something He owns, who are we to disagree? When God asks you to give, or to share, or to live a generous life in general, He's only asking you to manage the things He alone owns. We are always tempted to look at life in terms of what 'belongs' to us. "This is my time," or "this is my money." But, God calls us not to look at the world in terms of what we think is ours; but, in terms of all that is His. In so doing, we will have the right perspective on life and our material blessings and can live the generous and gracious lives to which He has called us.

Today's Generosity Challenge:
Look around your house and find something - regardless of value - you have been hanging onto for a year or more. Commit this item to prayer, asking the Lord who could really use this item. Then, with no fanfare, go and present it to them with simply, "The Lord asked me to bring this to you." Then, make a quick note in today's journal (http://GenerousLife. net/Day1) with their reaction to your obedience.

Day 2 - God is the provider of every good thing in your life

Matthew 7:11-12

[11] If you, then, though you are evil, know how to give good gifts to your children, how much more will your Father in heaven give good gifts to those who ask Him!
[12] So in everything, do to others what you would have them do to you, for this sums up the Law and the Prophets.

In Matthew 7, Jesus gives us an analogy for how we are to understand God. He says look at your fathers. These ordinary men, though they are sinners, though they are evil to the bone, though they are limited by time, energy, and motivation, even they know how to do good and generous things for their children. Imagine then, how good your heavenly Father is at giving good gifts to His spiritual children. He loves you more than any father could, after all He sent His son to die for you. He's not limited by time, money, or ability. Remember He's the all-powerful creator of the universe. So when God's children pray to Him, they understand that He will give them the absolute best, even if it's not what they were expecting.

Jesus then turns to how we treat others. We have two reasons to treat others well. The first is the most important and is based on what Jesus was just saying: God has been and will always be so good to us. He will give us only the best. If we are so well taken care of, we have the resources and motivation to love others as we have been loved. The second reason is especially practical. It is that however we treat others; we should also be okay with being so treated. Though none of us could say we deserve it, the best way we could ever want to be treated is how God has treated us all our lives.

If God has generously loved us, and if we desire to be treated generously, then how should we treat others? The right answer is the obvious answer; we should treat other people generously. Randy Alcorn said that as thunder follows lightning, giving follows grace. The one who has been so loved has a cup that is overflowing. The one who has been so loved is looking for opportunities to share this love and grace that has radically changed his or her life. They are able to give through their time, their treasure, their prayers. Once you have been shown God's grace, gratitude (of course; but, that's another book) and also generosity should be your response. And once you start looking for ways to be generous, you'll find that there are so many ways big and small. Let's close with this question to think about:

"Is it obvious to the people who know you that God has taken such good care of you?"

Today's Generosity Challenge:
Take a few minutes today and ask the Lord who needs some grace from you. Picture their face in your mind's eye. Rehearse what you need to say to them. Is it forgiveness, love, or understanding? Write it down in your journal so you don't forget your task. Now, set an appointment to meet with them and share what God has put in your heart. Remember to write down the date and time of your appointment and complete your journal with your observations of what the recipient said or did – and what God has shown you about His own grace for you at http://GenerousLife.net/Day2.

Day 3 - You are the manager of what God entrusts to you

Colossians 3: 17, 23, 24

[17] And whatever you do, whether in word or deed,
do it all in the name of the Lord Jesus,
giving thanks to God the Father through Him.
[23] Whatever you do, work at it with all your heart,
as working for the Lord, not for men,
[24] since you know that you will receive an inheritance
from the Lord as a reward.
It is the Lord Christ you are serving.

When we are working, whether at home, in school, or on the job, the way we work is going to be hugely influenced by one question: Who are you working for?

Is it your spouse and your children? Is it a difficult teacher? Is it a demanding boss?

Colossians 3 tells us that despite who we most immediately serve, in reality, we are serving Jesus. All those meals you cooked? You were serving Jesus. All those clients you helped? You were serving Jesus. All those floors you mopped? That was for Jesus too.

This is both a strong encouragement and a huge responsibility. It is encouraging because we won't always think highly of the people we work for, so if we realize that in all things we can (and should) be serving God, we have the best motivation there could possibly be. On the other hand, if we're serving God in all we do, we can't just say certain parts of our lives are unimportant so long as we take care of the "spiritual" parts. You know that time you did a sloppy job and didn't care? Well, that was for Jesus. You remember that customer you wrongly offended; well you did that for Jesus, too.

This same idea goes for how generous you are in life.
When you are generous, you are generous for Jesus.
When you are cheap, you are cheap for Jesus, as well.

Martin Luther said; people go through three conversions, heart, head, and pocketbook. His point was that we have such difficulty giving from our finances that it takes a change in perspective like being converted to start living generously with the wealth God has given us. But, this is not simply a call to give away a bunch of stuff; but, it is to realize that in so doing, you can serve God. Don't live generously because someone is trying to make you feel guilty. God won't be at all impressed by your coerced "generosity." Be generous to people because you are grateful to God for your salvation. Then go ahead; go be generous for Jesus.

Today's Generosity Challenge:
Before you head out today, ask the Lord to give you a new mindset for today's tasks. And no matter how menial, to show you how each is a task unto Him. Then, before the day is over, write down how you saw your day differently at http://GenerousLife.net/Day3.

Day 4 - The Lord watches your generosity

2 Corinthians 8:12
[12] For if the willingness is there, the gift is acceptable
according to what one has,
not according to what he does not have.

People are often grouped as "glass half-full" people or "glass half-empty" people. The glass half-full people are the optimists, always seeing what is good about a situation. The glass half-empty people are the pessimists, the ones who, instead of seeing what is good, only see what is wrong or missing. When God looks at your generosity, how does He see your glass? Do you think He looks at all the ways you could have done more or could have done better?

Many people experience huge amounts of guilt and anxiety because they don't think they are doing enough for God. They fear He isn't happy with them. But, the Scriptures tell us that God looks at the offerings His children bring graciously and generously. When a child makes a drawing for a parent, they come and say, "Look what I made you!" All you might see are a bunch of squiggly lines of crayon; but, when told it is a picture of the two of you playing outside, or a pony, or a million different things, no parent looks at the child and says, "Well this is sure a poor drawing; but, I guess I'll take it." Rather, because that picture is from your own child, it is cherished. And the next thing you know, you have a refrigerator covered with drawings that only look vaguely like what they are supposed to be.

Likewise, when God's children bring an offering to God made in love and eagerness, 2 Corinthians 8:12 says that God is well pleased with that offering. He doesn't judge His children according to all the things they never were or never accomplished. Rather, because they are His own spiritual children He receives the offering they bring.

If you are one of God's redeemed children, live generously toward God, in ways both large and small, and know that God is pleased by that action.

Today's Generosity Challenge:

Today is a two-part challenge; first prayerfully consider how you can do something for someone that is small; but, meaningful. Then, pray for something really sacrificial, something big that will cost you. Now, ask the Lord to present total strangers before you that your can live generously for them with these two challenges. Then tonight, before you go to bed, write down your observations and how your generosity was received. Journal your challenge here at http://GenerousLife.net/Day4. As your eyes close, ask the Lord to remind you of His generosity towards you, in the big things and the small things.

Day 5 - Don't be prideful
about your generosity

Deuteronomy 8:17-18

[17] You may say to yourself, "My power and the strength of my hands have produced this wealth for me."
[18] But, remember the LORD your God, for it is He who gives you the ability to produce wealth, and so confirms His covenant, which He swore to your forefathers, as it is today.

Romans 11:35

[35] "Who has ever given to God, that God should repay him?"

It feels good to serve the Lord. To be in His service is the highest privilege a person could receive. People in the world will do all sorts of things to work with someone important: maybe a Hollywood executive, a professional athlete, a great artist, or an influential thinker. It is an opportunity to learn and to be acquainted with someone of particular greatness. Maybe somewhere down the line, they will get one of those pictures with the person, standing side by side shaking hands and smiling for the camera. Maybe they'll have a great story of what it was to sit down across the table and have a conversation over dinner with this person: anything that makes that person more familiar and makes us more familiar to that person. Now think of this: we serve the King of All Creation and He knows us by name! We have much to feel good about!

One of the sad things about human beings is that we can mess up absolutely anything. For example, someone's generosity might be so used by God that they begin to grow proud. Not proud of God's great works; but, proud of their role in those great works. They might think, "Wow, look at me, I sure am one generous person."

Anytime we are tempted to such a thing we can remind ourselves of the truths presented in passages like Deuteronomy 8:17-18 or Romans 11:35 and what they teach, specifically, that everything we have, God has given us. The money in your bank account? God gave it to you. The job that earned that money? God gave you that, too. The skills that got you the job? God gave you when He made you. The education that got you the skills that got you the job? ... You get the point.

We become prideful when we start thinking that we are able to do "good" on, and by, own capability. Only when we realize that God has given us everything we have that enables us to live generously, we can see that God alone gets the glory. Like a mother who lets their child "help" with cooking a meal, the mother did all the really important things that made the meal taste good. In the same way with living generously, it is God who is accomplishing good. He just lets us participate.

Today's Generosity Challenge:
This one will be difficult. Through prayer, ask the Lord which of your attempts of a more generous life have you done this week out of your own desires or pride. Now, go to that recipient of your generosity and repent. Admit you gave for the wrong reason and you're sorry. Ask them how you can make it up to them. Be sure to journal their response here at http://GenerousLife.net/Day5.

Day 6 - Don't trust in riches, trust in God

Matthew 6:33
*[33] But, seek first his kingdom and his righteousness,
and all these things will be given to you as well.*

Money is a huge issue for people. But, you know what? It's actually not a very big issue to God. You see God owns everything. Everything in the world is His. God has never experienced a time when He wanted something; but couldn't do it because He didn't have enough money. Really, it seems like the main reason God is concerned with money is because we are so concerned with it.

We are concerned with money for a whole host of reasons. Mainly, because money is what enables us to eat, have a place to sleep, and pay for the things we need or want. Because money is so important to us, we also become very focused on who or what provides money for us. Whether it is a boss, the government, the stock market, our retirement plan, or any other source, we get so focused on these that we start forgetting that ultimately it is God who provides all for us.

The current economy has affected everyone. But, one group that is especially affected is the young adults. These people have never seen any other downturn in the economy. Most of their life has been lived during times of prosperity and success, and their lives were easier as a result. It is a very rattling thing to experience a downturn for the first time; to see that jobs grow scarce and realize that you don't or won't have the freedom, finances, and/or opportunity that you once had or might have had.

What people of any age need to remember in times like this is that it is God who will provide. We don't need better bosses, government, stock markets, or jobs. As Jesus said in Matthew 6:33: God knows what we need. He will not forget us. What we need to do, especially when times look bleak, is seek first God's kingdom and His righteousness, and our generous God will take care of all the rest.

Today's Generosity Challenge:

Today is a little different; it's about a longer commitment to others and their long-term success. If someone does not immediately come to mind, ask your Pastor's advice; but, find someone who has been particularly impacted by the economy, lost their house or job and ask them to meet with you for a cup of coffee. During that time together, ask them if you can come along side of them as a servant, a personal assistant, to be with them for the sole reason of helping them plan to get back on their feet. Then, of course, write down the plan here at http://GenerousLife.net/Day6.

Day 7 - Riches can deceive you

1 Timothy 6:9-10
⁹ People who want to get rich fall into temptation and a trap
and into many foolish and harmful desires
that plunge men into ruin and destruction.
¹⁰ For the love of money is a root of all kinds of evil.
Some people, eager for money, have wandered
from the faith and pierced themselves with many griefs.

Money solves a lot of problems. Need a new house? Bills you need to pay? Things you'd like to do? Money makes those kinds of things possible. Because money is legitimately useful, people will go to great ends to get it. The danger comes when we begin to think money is more important than it really is and begin to live our lives as if getting rich is a worthwhile life goal. What would you give up for riches? Is money worth a relationship with a friend? Is it worth your health? Is it worth the faith you profess in God?

If asked these sorts of questions point blank, none of us would likely say that money could be worth all those things. But, in practice, we often give up the most valuable things in our lives because we are pursuing money. 1 Timothy 6:9-10 describes the harm we will do to ourselves for money. Every day, life proves the Bible's point. Bit by bit we invest more of ourselves into the desire and pursuit of money. And as we dedicate our energies and affections to riches, we take them away from places they should be. We don't pray as we should, or study God and His word, we neglect our family, or we stop taking care of our health. And then one day, we realize that all the money we have amassed hasn't made us happy. In fact, while we've been trying to buy happiness, we've been deeply unhappy all along. When money distracts us and leads us away from God and the precious things in our lives, we have truly been deceived.

How can we avoid this deception? We need to remember always what money is actually good for. For example, money is good for taking care of physical needs. On the other hand, money cannot fill the deepest need of your soul which is to be reconciled to its Creator. Money is good for showing generosity to God and to others. Money cannot; however, buy you God's love or the true love of others. Keep God and money in their proper place in your life and God will bless you in yours.

Today's Generosity Challenge:

Please take out your personal bank statements for the last 6 months and make a simple survey. Count each time you have eaten out (coffee, too), bought goodies, spent money on entertainment, and purchased gifts for yourself or others, or any other indulgence regardless of amount. Write this number down in your journal. Now do the same thing (regardless of amount) for each time your expenditures were for blessing others financially, or by giving gifts to your church, or to charities. Just by the number of transactions, which is the greater number? Now write a short action plan on your observations and what priorities need to be readjusted. Journal here at http://GenerousLife.net/Day7.

Day 8 - Train your children to be generous

Psalm 78: 4-7

*4 We will not hide them from their children; we will tell
the next generation the praiseworthy deeds of the LORD,
His power, and the wonders He has done.
5 He decreed statutes for Jacob and established the law in Israel,
which He commanded our forefathers to teach their children,
6 so the next generation would know them, even the children yet to be
born, and they in turn would tell their children.
7 Then they would put their trust in God and would not forget His deeds
but, would keep His commands.*

In passages like this one in Psalm 78, the people of Israel were told to pass along the things they experienced of the Lord. They were to tell of His salvation, His mighty works, and how those things affected them in the present. Though we live in a different time and under different circumstances, parents have a similar responsibility today. Where Israel was to tell of their great rescue from slavery in the house of Egypt, today we tell of the great rescue from sin and death that Christ accomplished. And where Israel taught their children how to live a life of faith and worship in accordance to the Law, parents today teach their children how to live a life of generosity in light of the wealth that has been lavished out upon them in the Gospel.

Parents have the opportunity and responsibility to raise their children to live godly lives. It is an opportunity because they have the chance to raise their children in righteousness and to guide them away from the mistakes they themselves made in their own lives. It is a responsibility – a stewardship of lives – in that they are called to pass along the teachings of righteousness and godliness they have learned from the Scriptures. One way to do this is in teaching children, by word and practice, what it means to live generously in light of God's remarkable salvation. For better or for worse, children learn from their parents, both from what they hear them say and from what they see them do. Children learn from parents the way they are, or are not, willing to sacrifice for others. They learn from their parents how to be, or not to be, hospitable. They learn from their parents' things that will shape their perspective for the rest of their lives.

Do your children value generosity? Do they know the joy of making someone else happy? Do they know the satisfaction of giving to meet someone else's needs? Your example could set them on a path of generosity that blesses people for years to come. The example you set in your generosity could be multiplied in all the lives of all the people your child will encounter for the rest of their life. Enjoy the privilege. Cherish the responsibility.

Today's Generosity Challenge:

Start a discussion around the breakfast table this morning (or the dinner table tonight or even via an email, if your children are grown and out of the house) and ask them to define generosity. Write down their answers for Day 8 here at http://GenerousLife.net/Day8. Prayerfully, consider what they understand intuitively and in what areas do you need to teach your family generously.

Day 9 - Be content with God's daily provision

Ecclesiastes: 5:10

[10] *Whoever loves money never has money enough; whoever loves wealth is never satisfied with his income.*
This too is meaningless.

Philippians 4:13

[13] *I can do all things through Him who strengthens me.*

Money is an elusive thing. Do you remember as a young child "saving up" for something you really wanted? Maybe it was a comic book. Maybe it was a doll. With a goal in mind you did your chores and saved up for what felt like forever. Finally, you bought it and the joy lasted all of one week. And then, it was time to save up for the next big thing. As you grew older, maybe then you saved up for a bicycle. After that maybe it was a car. Later on it was a home. Then it was retirement. As we get older the price tags just get bigger and bigger, don't they?

Now this isn't a problem if you have kept money in a right place in your life. You work for a wage and you spend it to live your life, that's normal. There's nothing wrong with paying your bills. But, what if you've started to live and work just to make money? Ecclesiastes 5:10 teaches the danger of this is that if you've come to love money, you're never going to have enough. You'll never be satisfied, because money never can satisfy. Instead of truly living life, you will be living out a balance sheet. Everything has a dollar figure, but, nothing has value.

The Bible also teaches that the only path to contentment is the one that runs solely through Jesus Christ. Once we have found forgiveness and reconciliation in him, we find that we can be content in any circumstance, whether rich or poor. Furthermore, once we have learned to find our contentment in Christ alone, we find ourselves able to live generously in a way that we were never able to before. While money was our joy and treasure, we couldn't bear to part with it. Once Christ became our treasure, we realized we were not only able, but, even desiring to be generous to the glory of the Lord. In fact, by giving up worldly treasure, we can come to gain heavenly treasure. In the matters of the soul and heart, more money is never the solution.

Today's Generosity Challenge:

Today, I want you to be introspective. In a listening prayer, ask the Lord to reveal to you how to attribute the importance of things by a dollar figure. What circumstances challenge your contentment? Then write down what the Holy Sprit reveals to you here at http://GenerousLife.net/Day9.

Day 10 - There are dangerous consequences in living only for pleasure

Ecclesiastes: 7:4
*⁴ The heart of the wise is in the house of mourning,
but, the heart of fools is in the house of pleasure.*

There are many pleasurable things in the world: whether it's a trip to the beach, a great dinner, a comfortable bed, or just a hot shower. One of the ways we see the wonders of God's creation is by seeing that God has truly blessed us with so many pleasing things in this world. But, pleasure, by itself, can never satisfy for long.

If we only pursue pleasure, what satisfaction will we have? Imagine the person who only eats cookies because cookies bring them the most pleasure. Will they be happy for long? Imagine a person who never attends to the needs of their spouse because they only pursue personal pleasures. Will they have a deep and enduring relationship? Imagine a person who neglects faith, love and righteousness to pursue a shortsighted life of passing excitement. Will they have joy in God?

This verse in Ecclesiastes 7:4 teaches that the heart of fools is in the house of pleasure. The reason this is so foolish is because to invest one's life in pleasure will so obviously leave one wanting for more. It is only living a life that keeps our own pleasure in proportion to the whole of the Christian life will we find joy. A misunderstanding of how much pleasure really makes us happy is a big reason we don't live generously. We don't live generously because we fear that if we do we will be giving up what makes us truly happy. Once we realize that it is Christ in whom we find lasting joy, we realize that our soul's eternal pleasure is tied to finding ways to please him. We realize that in fact, if we are not seeking to please God, we're not really happy at all. You see we flee from a life of selfish pleasure because in the end it is poisonous to our soul. On the other hand, we flock to a life of generosity, because ultimately it is ever-lasting happiness.

Today's Generosity Challenge:

How do you please God daily in order for you to know what makes you feel truly happy? What are the best ways you please God? How do you know? Write them down now. Though prayer, ask the Lord how can you focus on those activities in an ever-increasing way. Then, write out a plan in real tangible ways by journaling here at http://GenerousLife.net/Day10.

Day 11 - You must serve God with money, not the other way around

Matthew 6:24

24"No one can serve two masters. Either he will hate the one and love the other, or he will be devoted to the one and despise the other. You cannot serve both God and Money.

A young Christian, full of passion and zeal, once said in his heart, I am going to make a lot of money so I can be a huge help to the kingdom of God. I may not be the one who goes on the missions, but, I can pay for those who will. So, aspiring to great financial gain, he dedicated himself to college and the pursuit of a degree that could make his dream happen. He was very good at what he did and succeeded in landing a good job after graduation. But, something went wrong.

At some point, he stopped wanting to give. While he was a student and working part time, he found giving to be very easy, for the amounts he faithfully gave were not large amounts. Once he began earning larger amounts of money, he found it hard to give in the same manner he once had. The large checks he wrote in the beginning he only did so with great difficulty. Over time, he found that he would much rather keep the money than give it away. After a long journey, he ended up doing exactly the opposite of what he had hoped to do. His generosity had faded into a tight-fisted cheapness; his passionate heart had been burdened down by the worries of the money he earned.

What happened to this man? Jesus taught in Matthew 6:24 that a Christian cannot have two masters. If he tries, he will only truly serve one of his masters, the other he will despise. Specifically, Jesus said that you cannot serve both God and money. In this case, the man stopped serving God and began serving money. At some point, he decided that he would rather have all the money he was earning than serve the God he set out to please. Money is a good thing when used in accordance with God's will. When we begin to seek out money without submitting its use to God and his word, then we begin to let money be our master.

Many people mistakenly think God is there to help us get

wealthy. This is the greatest misunderstanding of who God is. What we need to realize is that God will not be used to make us money; but, money can be used to honor God.

Today's Generosity Challenge:

Have you ever made a similar statement; "God, if you provide for me in this way, I promise I will serve you this way." What is the problem with this approach? If this is you, today I want you to write an apology to the Lord. You can journal here at this link http://GenerousLife.net/Day11. Be specific, and repent.

Day 12 - Live for your Heavenly Home, not for this life

Hebrews 11:10

10 For he was looking forward to the city with foundations, whose architect and builder is God.

Matthew 6:19-20

19 "Do not store up for yourselves treasures on earth, where moth and rust destroy, and where thieves break in and steal.
20 But, store up for yourselves treasures in heaven, where neither moth nor rust destroys, and where thieves do not break in or steal;

What if I told you I'd give you a $100 bill for every one dollar of monopoly money that you gave me? This would be quite a good deal for you wouldn't it? You would be saying, "I can give up something that is not really worth anything, and in exchange I get receive back something that is really worth a decent amount."

God asks us to view life in a similar way. What He says is this: I have entrusted you with temporary and earthly resources. Your time, your energy, your finances, these are the kinds of blessings He gives us on earth. What God also says, though, is: based on how you handle these temporary blessings; I am willing to give you abundantly more in heaven. If God's children are willing to live generously with what God has given them and to not shrink away from the roles God has called them to play, then truly they can expect treasure in heaven that makes any earthly goods pale in comparison.

Jim Elliot said, "He is no fool who gives up what he cannot keep, to gain that which he cannot lose."

In your heart do you believe what Jesus said in Matt 19:29 that whatever He calls you to give up in this world you can expect 100 times as much in return in heaven? This is not a simple thing; but, understand this: Jesus is not saying what you have in this world is worthless. Rather, He is saying that even with how much your worldly things are worth, He can give you so, so much more. We are called to live generously, not

because of what we expect in this life; but, because of what God prom-
ises us in heaven. Life is not so simple as a game of monopoly. But, then
again, the reward that awaits us is infinitely more glorious than a mere
$100 bill.

Today's Generosity Challenge:

  Okay this is a big one. While you were reading today's devotion,
what came to mind to give up? Does it frighten you? Is it a car, a large
sum of money, or a piece of property? Through prayer, if you think this
is something with which to bless someone else, THEN DO IT! Be sure to
write down your experience, your feeling of fear, and the blessings at
http://GeneorusLife.net/Day12. Return to this day often.

Day 13 - Generosity – proportionate to how you have been materially blessed

Luke 12:48
[48] From everyone who has been given much, much will be demanded; and from the one who has been entrusted with much, much more will be asked."

Imagine a front desk attendant at a charity opening mail. As she opens one of the envelopes, a wrinkled five-dollar bill falls out with a note attached to it. The note reads simply, "This is all I have to give you, I'm sorry it can't be more. Yours truly, Mr. Smith" The attendant is touched by the effort. True, five dollars won't accomplish a lot at the charity; but it appears that the benefactor has sacrificed tremendously to be able to give to the work of the charity. It is this kind of sacrifice, she thinks to herself, from which we can all learn.

Now imagine that later, while telling her co-workers of the touching deed she mentions Mr. Smith's name, and one of her co-workers says, "Wait, isn't that Mr. Smith the multi-millionaire?" Suddenly, what went from a very touching and inspirational deed becomes not only less spectacular; but, also even deceitful and pathetic. The rich man, not wanting to actually part with his wealth decided that he would just made it look like he had. What was once so commendable suddenly became downright reproachable.

The Bible teaches that in life, those to whom much has been given will have much expected of them (Luke 12:48). There is no percentage or exact figure in the New Testament for what a Christian is to give; but there is certainly an expectation that we give proportionate to what we have. If you have not yet learned to live generously with what you have, consider whether, perhaps, the Lord may want you to change the way you live and the way you give. I can't tell you exactly what you should do because the Bible doesn't say so; but, if you are a believer and the Spirit is pricking your conscience, maybe it's time you stopped sending wrinkled five dollar bills and stepped forward to the generous life your God has made you capable of living.

Today's Generosity Challenge:

Today, I want you to view your checkbook or bank statement again. This time calculate the last six to twelve months expenditures versus giving before you started your giving journey. What is your real percentage? No cheating – the real number of givings of cash vs. all other gross expenditures. Now, take a big post-it note and put it on your refrigerator. Oh, and remember to write it down, too, at http://GenerousLife.net/Day13.

Day 14 - Ordinary people, extraordinary generosity

Mark 14:3, 8-9

*³ While he was in Bethany, reclining at the table in the home
of a man known as Simon the Leper, a woman came
with an alabaster jar of very expensive perfume,
made of pure nard. She broke the jar and poured the perfume
on His head...*
*⁸ She did what she could. She poured perfume on my body
beforehand to prepare for my burial.*
*⁹ I tell you the truth, wherever the gospel is preached
throughout the world, what she has done will also be told,
in memory of her."*

Do you believe you are insignificant? Do you look at yourself sometimes and wonder how you could ever amount to anything worthwhile? Many of us share these doubts and misgivings. We know ourselves along with our weaknesses. We feel aimless, sometimes we even feel useless. The Gospel of Mark tells of one encounter that provides an unexpected encouragement to us.

In Mark 14, days before Jesus is crucified, he is having dinner in the house of a man named Simon. At some point in the meal, an unnamed woman enters, breaks an expensive bottle of perfume and pours the contents on Jesus' head. In our culture, that would be an especially bizarre occurrence, not to mention you might reek of perfume for days. But, Jesus sees it for the generous act that it was. Perfume was a costly commodity, worth almost a year's worth of wages, and Jesus tells them that this unnamed woman has done a good deed and has anointed His body for His burial to come. Moreover, He says that this woman's act of generosity and faith will be remembered wherever the Gospel is preached.

Isn't it remarkable that this ordinary and unnamed woman performed one of the most famous acts of generosity in all of history? We are not told that this woman was a famous philanthropist or even an especially upright person. We are not told whether she had been doing her daily devotions faithfully throughout her life or that she was far from perfect. What we are given to remember and learn from is that this woman, though ordinary, was capable of performing extraordinary generosity to our Lord.

Few people might have a year's worth of wages to give away; but, every person is capable of this kind of generosity. Jesus does not look at your generosity and add up in his head to decide if it is commendable or not. Rather, if your generosity springs from a heart grateful for the salvation Jesus accomplished, then your generosity can be extraordinary as well.

Today's Generosity Challenge:

You need a vision, a generosity vision for your life. Here is how you get one. Take the time to get away alone, today. No TV, radio, MP3, or conversation. Along with your Bible, sit down and ask the Lord for a vision of what He wants you to do with your life that will make a BIG difference in someone's else's life. Something beyond you, something GOD-sized, something a little scary. Once you have it, I want you to go to our website and tell the world here at http://GenerousLife.net/Day14. If you do, we'll send you an action plan on how to begin to put your idea into action.

Day 15 - Be cautious of greed

2 Corinthians 9: 6-7

⁶ Remember this: Whoever sows sparingly will also reap sparingly, and whoever sows generously will also reap generously.
⁷ Each man should give what he has decided in his heart to give, not reluctantly or under compulsion, for God loves a cheerful giver.

Christians tend to like rules. They like to know exactly what is expected in any given situation. Should I reach out to help this person? How much should I give? How long should I pray? What specific things should I do every day to please God?

These aren't bad questions, not at all. In fact, often these desires spring from our desire to please God in every way, yet not knowing exactly how. The problem with our love of rules and specifics is that the Bible doesn't always give us specifics. The Bible, in many cases, tells us to do something; but leaves it to us to figure out how.

Take the command of "loving your neighbor as yourself." This is a powerful and important teaching of Jesus; but what does that look like? How do we do that exactly? Is it opening doors for people? Is it calling them up to see how they are? Is it inviting people over for dinner? Is it going to another country to help? The Scriptures don't specifically tell us. Christians are meant to study Scripture, pray, search their hearts, and then do what they can in a good conscience.

2 Corinthians 9 speaks about giving. In it Paul says that we should give not reluctantly or because someone is forcing us to. Rather, we are supposed to decide in our heart what to do and give cheerfully. God does not want our generosity to be out of guilt. He wants generosity motivated by love. Sometimes you might not have much; but, you can still be generous with a cheerful heart. Sometimes you might have a lot in terms of resources, God calls you likewise to be generous with a cheerful heart. The amount of time or treasure you are generous with is not God's main point. For God, numbers are not the issue. God wants His children first to be generous from the heart, and then the specifics can work themselves out after that.

41

Today's Generosity Challenge:

One simple question: When does emotion dictate your giving? There's not really a right or wrong answer here; just describe it in writing here at http://GenerousLife.net/Day15. What have you learned?

Day 16 - God has good works for you to do in your lifetime

Ephesians 2:10

[10] For we are God's workmanship,
created in Christ Jesus to do good works,
which God prepared in advance for us to do.

"What am I doing in life?" This is a question many people ask a many points in their lives. "Why am I here?" "What is my purpose?" Purpose drives us; it helps us understand why we get out of bed each day. When we have an answer to that question of "why," then we understand how to make it through both good and bad times. If we don't have an answer to this question, then life will discourage us, it will confuse us, and it will leave us searching desperately for meaning.

The Bible tells us our purpose is in life: We are alive to glorify God. Paul tells us in Ephesians 2:10 that one of the ways God's children can glorify Him is by doing the good works He has planned out for us. Paul tells us that we were designed to do good works; it is what we are meant for. And over the course of our new life in Christ, God has laid out for us a whole plan of good works we get to do.

So Christians are meant to live out these good works. What does that mean? What exactly is a good work? Well, look around you, who do you see every day? Are there things you know you could do to be a blessing to those around you? Assess yourself. What kinds of things do you know how to do? It can be anything from playing music ... to doing manual labor ... to practicing medicine. Maybe you are just a friendly person. Whatever your talents may be, you can be generous with them for someone who is in their need.

"Who?" you say? Look into your heart – what do you 'have a heart for?' Do you love children? The elderly? Do you have a heart to fight poverty or help in education? Pursue the things that God has put on your heart.

When we look at the world, we see there are so many good works that we can be doing. Every single day God has equipped you with

43

the purpose and ability to live the generous life you were made for.

Today's Generosity Challenge:

Go back and look at your entry from Day 13. Reflect back on that day's entry and through prayer write down how you have been uniquely prepared for such a God-sized vision at http://GenerousLife.net/Day16.

Day 17 - Some people are called to extravagant generosity

Acts 4:34-37

34 There were no needy persons among them. For from time to time, those who owned lands or houses sold them, brought the money from the sales
35 and put it at the apostles' feet, and it was distributed to anyone as he had need.
36 Joseph, a Levite from Cyprus, whom the apostles called Barnabas (which means Son of Encouragement),
37 sold a field he owned and brought the money and put it at the apostles' feet.

It's been one said that of the best reasons to buy real estate is because it is the only thing they're not making any more of it. This is a light-hearted way to note the importance of land. Residential real estate is one of the most significant purchases a person can make. Home owner-ship is so important to people that they will pay for that home for 30 years of their life! The home people live in is very commonly the most valuable possession they have.

The book of Acts records the growth and development of the church in the early days after Jesus ascended to heaven. In chapter 4 of this book, it describes how some believers went so far in their generosity that they were selling their houses and land in order to provide money for the church in its need. Just as it would be no small decision if you were to sell your home, or whatever you own that is most valuable, it was undoubtedly no small sacrifice for these believers either. So why did they do this? They saw a need and they felt called to be extravagantly generous to meet that need.

Not all generosity is extravagant. In fact, daily and regular gener-osity is a great Christian witness in and of itself. But, some people might have both the means and the calling to be extravagantly generous. Is that you? If you think the Spirit might be leading you to be generous in this way, do yourself a favor. Pray about it faithfully and seek the counsel of the Word of God and people you trust. Investigate the need and investigate what kind of generosity you might be able to show. If you after all this you still think you are called to be generous in an extravagant way, then go ahead and be generous unto the Lord.

Are you balking at the decision because it would be such a large act of generosity? It's totally understandable if there are some nerves involved, big decisions are like that. Sit down and think it through again. If you already have the desire, if it is not a foolish choice, and if God through his word and through prayer seems to be confirming your desire to be generous, then perhaps, the only way you are going to be happy is if you follow His call to live generously. And lastly, remember this: Extravagant generosity is also a privilege. Few people in history have had the chance to support God's work with extravagant generosity. Go ahead and enjoy the opportunity before you!

Today's Generosity Challenge:

Go back to your challenge from day 12 and review it again. Did you follow through? If not, why not do it today? If you did: Congratulations! Now, do it again and allow the Lord to show himself faithful. This time I want you to go to http://GenerousLife.net/Day17 and write down your experience.

Day 18 - It is appropriate to ask people how you can help

Mark 10: 51-52

[51] *"What do you want me to do for you?" Jesus asked him.*
The blind man said, "Rabbi, I want to see."
[52] *"Go," said Jesus, "your faith has healed you."*
Immediately he received his sight and followed Jesus along the road.

There is so much we can learn from Jesus. Sometimes it is just astounding. In the tenth chapter of the Gospel of Mark, a blind man cries out to Jesus for mercy. Jesus calls the man over and asks, "What do you want me to do for you?" Let's remember that Jesus is the Son of God. I am sure that Jesus knew exactly how the blind man wanted to be helped. So why did He decide to ask the question?

On the one hand, Jesus is giving this blind man a chance to express his request in faith. In so doing, God is glorified and both the blind man's faith and the faith of all who watched would be increased. They would glorify God because of God's powerful answer to that prayer. We also remember that in relation to us, Jesus is not only our savior; He is also the best role model we could ever have. When we see how He lived, we desire to imitate and learn from Him.

When I see Jesus reaching out to this man and asking how He can help him, I look at my life and I think, "Maybe I, too, should be asking people how I can help them." See, none of us had all the knowledge and power that Jesus has, so if we are going to figure out how we are to love our neighbor as ourselves, we are going to have to ask some questions. Have you ever been having a really bad day; but you managed to act normal so no one knew something was wrong? Other people know how to do that, too. Maybe they won't let themselves be helped until someone comes to them and asks point blank how they can help them. Have you ever had a whole lot of stress in your life; but you managed to leave it at home rather than wear it on your sleeve wherever you went? Well, other people can do that one, too. Maybe the people you see all the time – who look like they're doing just fine – are really struggling.

Maybe you could vastly improve their lives through your generosity. I tell you what, there's only one way to find out.

Today's Generosity Challenge:

Again, find someone in your church to help. Not sure who? Ask your Pastor. Find someone with a health issue, a marital problem, or is a single parent. This time, find out what the one, breakthrough act of generosity could be for that person. And no matter how big or small – prayerfully find a way to succeed. Recruit others, have a fundraiser, think big – go for it. If God is for you, who could be against you? Oh yeah, write down your experiences, in detail. Don't leave anything out here at http://GenerousLife.net/Day18.

Day 19 - God blesses you financially so that you can bless others

Hebrews 6:10-11

[10] God is not unjust; He will not forget your work and the love you have shown Him as you have helped His people and continue to help them. [11] We want each of you to show this same diligence to the very end, in order to make your hope sure.

When children are little, they are learning new things virtually every single day. As they learn how to do new things, they also want to show their parents. This results in something like, "Look mommy, look daddy, look what I can do!" And this process repeats for about as many times as the parent has patience.

See, growing up is an exciting time. New discoveries are constantly being made. The child, not yet understanding concepts like humility or bragging, recognizes that they have made an accomplishment and they want to be sure that their parents know about it.

Living the Christian life, we are called to many moments of quiet generosity. We might even be called to act generously in ways that no one will ever know we had a part. Think how many things go on at church and you have no idea who does them! But, God is always watching. In Hebrews 6:10, the author says that God will never forget the love his children show Him as they help His people. Unlike people who have such short memories ("So, what have you done for me lately?"), God will never forget the times we loved Him by living generously toward others. That doesn't mean we go around saying, "Look at me, God, Look at me!" But, God is gracious in that He is pleased by all the various ways His people show themselves to be generous.

If you've ever wondered how to love God, well here's one great way: Go be generous to His people. Randy Alcorn once said, "Giving is a giant lever positioned on the fulcrum of this world, allowing us to move mountains in the next world. Because we give, eternity will be different - for others and for us." If you're rusty on your physics, we can say it this way: God's going to give His children huge credit in eternity for the generosity they show in this brief moment that is our life.

Today's Generosity Challenge:

Okay, this one is easy. Years ago, a man who I had been discipling gave me a tent out of the blue. That's right, a tent! Why a tent? Because he knew I loved backpacking and that I needed a new tent. He took the time and did the research to find just what I needed. It was the best personal gift I can remember receiving. So, today, I want you to go and bless your Pastor or another spiritual leader in your life that has spent their life pouring themselves into you. Be thoughtful and make it meaningful to them. Then be sure to journal the experience – and the reactions – at http://GenerousLife.net/Day19.

Day 20 - Living generously even when you're dead

Proverbs 13:22
22 A good man leaves an inheritance for his children's children;
but, a sinner's wealth is stored up for the righteous.

Proverbs 13:22 says that one of the generosities a good man can show is by leaving an inheritance, not just to his children; but, to his children's children. The idea is that this man, rather than spending all his resources on himself alone, chose to save his money so that it might bless people in ways he'll never see. It is quite a selfless act of generosity to conserve one's own use of resources and give them to future generations, and it is a practice that is to be commended.

Have you thought about how you can be generous for years after you are gone? This isn't just a question for the wealthy who might be able to pass along large sums of money to their family. No, this question applies to any kind of person. You might say, "I'm a pretty ordinary person, what can I possibly do?" You can live generously and pass on a legacy and model of generosity that will bless generations of descendants who will indirectly be blessed by your actions and attitude. You can generously pass along the wisdom and knowledge you have to younger generations. (All those mistakes have to add up to something!) If you are educated, maybe you can tutor. If you have been through lots of bad life decisions, maybe you can counsel people who might in danger of making the mistakes you made.

When you invest in the generations still to come, you have no way of knowing how greatly the Lord can multiply your generosity. Imagine if your generosity affects just two people. Now imagine that each of those people bless two more people. If God chooses, the ripple of your generosity could spread far beyond anything you could ever have imagined and farther into the future than you thought possible. Never underestimate the value of blessing the generations to come.

Today's Generosity Challenge:
Today, your challenge is to research, find and set an appoint-

ment with a financial planner. Even it you don't have what you feel is much of an estate to plan, do it anyway. I think you'll be surprised. Write down your surprises at http://GenerousLife.net/Day20.

Day 21 - Life is more than the things we own

Luke 12:23
³ Life is more than food, and the body more than clothes.

What makes for a full life? Is it the home we live in? Is it the car we drive or the vacations we've been on? Few people would think that their life is defined by their home, car, or vacations; yet, many people live their lives in this way. It's been said that those possessions we own eventually own us. That is to say, as we attain more and more of the belongings we desire, we can reach a point when the obligations attached to them begin to run our life. For example, a man who buys a sports car might spend all his time working to pay it off without ever getting on the road and enjoying the car he bought. What happens when our life is defined by all the stuff we own?

If this is you, I suggest two things:

- One, at the end of the day, when you put your head on the pillow, your possessions aren't actually satisfying your soul.
- And two, you are so absorbed in the world's things that you've completely lost sight of the fact that we are meant to live for so much more.

Hear how Jesus put it in Luke 12:23: "Life is more than food, and the body more than clothes."

If you are a child of God, you are not supposed to live a life that is only concerned with material things. You have a Father in heaven that gave His own Son to save you from your sins. He poured out indescribable wealth upon you and now you are one of His own!

People who come to believe that material things are the absolute best things we have in life are going to have an incredibly difficult time parting with those things. Once you realize that life is so much more than material things, you can live generously. In eternity, no one will care about what kind of car you drove or how many square feet your house was. But, one thing that will matter in eternity: Did you look beyond the world's "stuff" and live the generous life that God treasures?

Today's Generosity Challenge:

What did the research into a financial planner tell you about your approach to storing up treasures here on earth or in heaven? In your actual estate plan, what are you going to change, what will be your goal to give more? Write down your ideas at http://GenerousLife.net/Day21.

Day 22 - Being rich toward God

Luke 12:16-21

¹⁶ And He told them this parable: "The ground of a certain rich man produced a good crop.
¹⁷ He thought to himself, 'What shall I do? I have no place to store my crops.'
¹⁸ "Then he said, 'This is what I'll do. I will tear down my barns and build bigger ones, and there I will store all my grain and my goods.
¹⁹ And I'll say to myself, "You have plenty of good things laid up for many years. Take life easy; eat, drink and be merry."'
²⁰ "But, God said to him, 'You fool! This very night your life will be demanded from you. Then who will get what you have prepared for yourself?'
²¹ "This is how it will be with anyone who stores up things for himself; but, is not rich toward God."

In Luke Chapter 12:16-21, Jesus teaches this parable about a prosperous rich man. This man was so well off that he had to figure out where he was going to be able to fit all his crops and goods. So he says to himself, "I have so much food that the barns I have can't hold it all. I guess I'll just have to tear down my barns and build new ones." The rich man thought that once he stored up enough wealth that he would be able to depend on that wealth and live an easy and carefree life. You know how God responded? He answered, "You fool! This very night your life will be demanded from you. Then who will get what you have prepared for yourself?" And Jesus sums it all up by saying that this is how it will happen for the person who stores up things for themselves; but, is not rich toward God.

Now I don't know about you; but that story really hits me. We so often forget all about God because we're thinking so much about how to take care of ourselves. The way we handle our treasure, our energy and our time really reflects this.

Be honest, now – do you find yourself (as I do, more often than not) trying to figure out how much you "have to" give to God to just get by?

But, that's not what God made us for. You see; He gave His own Son to save us. The more we dwell on that, the more our hearts will overflow with gratitude. God has been so rich to us in the Gospel and while we can't ever repay Him for what he did, we can live gratefully in response. Whatever it is you have, go ahead, live richly toward God.

Today's Generosity Challenge:

In today's vernacular we don't build bigger barns, we "move up" to a bigger house, a nicer car, more extravagant vacations. But, is that what God wants you to do? How can you stop the upward trend in the big things and small things? After all, if we are striving to a Generous Life, we need to be scaling down to bless others. Please journal your ideas for scaling down here at http://GenerousLife.net/Day22.

Day 23 - Generosity in the big picture

Proverbs 11:24-25
[24] One man gives freely, yet gains even more;
another withholds unduly; but, comes to poverty.
[25] A generous man will prosper;
he who refreshes others will himself be refreshed.

Generosity is a surprising thing. You see, a lot of people think they can't be generous because if they are they won't have enough for themselves. If they give away their money, they won't be able to buy things for themselves. If they give away their time or their energy, there won't be enough left over to take care of themselves. What's surprising is that God's word says just about the complete opposite of that!

Proverbs 11: 24-25 says that the man who gives freely gains even more. The world often teaches that we have to look out only for ourselves if we are to get by. "Just take care of #1," we hear. But, the Bible says, "Don't do that!" Looking only to yourself will sometimes make you an extra buck; but, all those extra bucks will leave you poorer in the end.

I'm not going to sugar coat it: Being generous isn't always easy and true generosity will cost you something.

If you give freely to God and to people, it will mean you will be giving up something you could have kept for yourself. But, the reason the Bible can say you will gain even more is because Christians live in light of eternity. When Christ rose from the grave, believers were given new life. And in that new life, the rules have totally changed.

If we want to take care of ourselves, we take care of others. If we want to find our life, we need to first lose it in Christ.

We all know what it's like to shrink back from a chance to be generous. It's not easy because it doesn't feel natural.

But, know this, when Jesus was on earth teaching, he didn't tell us to expect treasure on earth, he said to expect treasure in heaven. When it comes down to it, God will bless your generosity for all eternity.

Today's Generosity Challenge:

Reflect of the last 22 challenges you have tackled in this journey. Be honest, which one have you shrunk back from or ignored? Write them down at http://GenerousLife.net/Day23, and then, through prayer, go before the Lord and ask Him what's holding you back. Write those answers down here, as well.

Day 24 - Why be generous?

1 Timothy 6:18-19
*[18] Command them to do good, to be rich in good deeds,
and to be generous and willing to share.
[19] In this way, they will lay up treasure for themselves as a firm
foundation for the coming age, so that they may take
hold of the life that is truly life.*

When people think of Christianity, they often already know a lot about its rules and its standards. They know so much about the dos and don'ts; but they often don't know much about the bigger question, "Why?"

It should be no surprise to you that the Bible commands us to live generously. 1 Timothy 6 commands us to be rich in good deeds, to be generous and willing to share. But, do you know what reason Paul gives for living this kind of generous life? Whatever the reason is, it is going to make a huge difference in our ability and desire to live out this command.

Some people think God tells us to do things just for cold obedience – as though God just wants to see if you'll do something difficult and self-sacrificing for Him. While one of the biggest ways we love God is by obeying Him, God is so generous to us that He also gives us huge rewards to encourage us to obey.

The reason Paul gives for our good deeds and generosity is two-fold:

First, he says that by living this way we will lay up treasure for the coming age. In living generously we are actually storing up eternal treasure. It's like a spiritual investment plan; invest a little now to receive way more in heaven!

Second, Paul says that we will be taking hold of the life that is truly life. By living generously in light of eternity, we are giving up temporary things like our treasure or our time, the things some people think are the essentials of life, and in exchange we get to have true and full life from God, the kind of life God wants most for us. So when God calls us to obey and live generously, we do so knowing that what He offers us is so much greater than what He calls us to give up.

Today's Generosity Challenge:

Again let's reflect on the last 23 Generosity Challenges. What have you learned about the "why" of being generous? Write down your thoughts here at http://GenerousLife.net/Day24. Now, how has it begun to change you?

Day 25 - None of your stuff is coming with you to eternity

1 Timothy 6:6-8
⁶ But, godliness with contentment is great gain.
⁷ For we brought nothing into the world,
and we can take nothing out of it.
⁸ But, if we have food and clothing, we will be content with that.

Anyone who has ever moved has had this thought: "Wow, I can't believe I have this much stuff!" The reason this is especially clear is because you, in some manner or another, will have to pick up and move every single thing you have. Every box or armful means one more trip, one more trip up the stairs, one more trip down the hall; it makes for a lot of trips.

One good thing about moving is it also causes us to evaluate what we really need. We start to see what is really important and what is just 'stuff.' The important things we keep, the stuff we get rid of. It's a great process like that.

The Bible teaches us that in light of eternity, and our possessions are really just stuff. Paul notes in 1 Timothy Chapter 6 that we didn't bring anything into the world. And you know what? We're not taking anything out of the world either. Once we realize that none of our possessions will last into eternity, we have a new freedom.

If none of our stuff is eternal, then we don't have to treat it like it is so important. In light of eternity, it becomes insignificant if we have the newest or the nicest things.

And let's go even further. If we don't get to keep any of our possessions, it's a whole lot easier to be generous with them, isn't it? Just like it is easy to give away an old piece of furniture you were getting rid of anyway, it becomes so much easier to give away the things we think "belong" to us because, well, God's getting rid of them when Christ returns anyway. When we live within the light of eternity, generosity just makes sense.

Today's Generosity Challenge:

With your family, take a real inventory of everything in your house you haven't used in the last 18 months. Everything – clothes, furniture, toys, even (or especially) including everything in storage. Now, call the paper and announce a yard sale. That's right; sell it all – be courageous – sell all of it. Then take all the proceeds and first pay off any debt you may have, starting with your credit cards. Then, call you favorite charity and donate everything that didn't sell. If by some chance you still have a few dollars left, drop that in the offering box at your church. Be sure to write down how freeing this experience was at http://GenerousLife.net/Day25.

Day 26 - Generosity and Hospitality: More than writing a check

Romans 12:13
*¹³ Share with God's people who are in need.
Practice hospitality.*

You know, I talk about generosity a lot. One thing I've noticed is that when people hear about generosity, they think I'm just talking about money. But, the truth is, generosity includes a lot more than money!

Believe it or not, for some people it is one of the simplest tasks in the world to write someone a check. What do I mean by that? Well, for some people – and they don't even have to be rich – writing a check is a quick way to show someone you care without having to really invest in that person. All they do is fill out that check, tear it off and give it to the person and they go away feeling like they did a generous thing.

Did you know it is far more difficult for this kind of person to actually spend time with a person caring for them? While for many people, money is the most expensive thing they could give away –for others, it is a lot harder to give of their time and their energy.

One example where the Bible addresses this is in Romans Chapter 12. Here, Paul teaches that we are to be hospitable toward others. True hospitality means that as you invest in someone else's life, you also invite them into yours. When you have someone over, perhaps making them dinner or something like that, you are showing that person love and generosity that money could never communicate.

Generosity isn't any one thing. If you've received God's generosity in the Gospel, then your whole life is going to reflect that generosity.

Today's Generosity Challenge:

I'd like to challenge you in this way: invite someone over for a meal. Let people into your life and invest in theirs. And as you go out looking to be generous to someone else, I'll bet you that you end up getting blessed in the process, too. Write down those blessings here http://GenerousLife.net/Day26.

Day 27 - Blessed be the generous

Proverbs 22:9
⁹ A generous man will himself be blessed, for he shares his food with the poor.

Generosity is often portrayed as what you do for other people. When someone needs a ride, you go pick him or her up. When someone is lonely, you reach out to him or her. When there is a financial need, you see what you can do to meet it. Generosity becomes defined as what you do for others.

Now there's no doubt, helping people is a big part of generosity – and the person so helped is greatly blessed. But, what people don't always realize is that generosity is also a blessing to the giver. Proverbs 22 says that a generous man will himself be blessed. That means that the generous person isn't just the one blessing others; but in that generosity the giver will also receive blessing. This blessing might come in different ways; but one sure way it will come is in the eyes of the Lord. In living generously, you will be pleasing Him and storing up eternal blessing for yourself. Know that God smiles on your generosity, is itself, a blessing.

Throughout their lives, Christians look at themselves and ask, "How can I grow as a believer?" As they pursue living out the Gospel, they work on praying more faithfully, on studying the Word, on working on their character and the way they react to sin and temptation. There are all these critical ways to pursue our faith.

But, one way that people don't always think of is through generosity. God will bless you and grow you as a Christian when you seek to live generously in His name. So when you are looking to please God and grow, definitely invest yourself in prayer and the Word and good things like that. But, don't forget about generosity, after all, generosity is just one more tool God is using to make you like Christ.

Today's Generosity Challenge:
Let's talk about the little things. Who do you know that could use a ride to church, to the doctor, or to a hair appointment? What single

mom could use an oil change or some household repair? How could you come along side someone that just needs a little something that we usually just take for granted? Now, go and do it. Afterwards, write down the effect it had on them and you at http://GenerousLife.net/Day27

Day 28 - How to give generously

1 Corinthians 16:2
*² On the first day of every week, each one of you should set aside
a sum of money in keeping with his income, saving it up,
so that when I come no collections will have to be made.*

When you consider your generosity and your giving to God, do you feel like you have a pretty good sense of how to please God in this way? You can easily see it going at least two different ways.

- Some might give next to nothing and then pat themselves on the back thinking they really did a great job.
- Others might give a huge amount; but feel guilty that they haven't made God happy.

And there are a lot of other types of people that might exist; but it's an important question: What does God expect of us in terms of our giving?

I think we can learn a helpful lesson from Paul's first letter to the Corinthian Church. In Chapter 16, Paul talks about a collection he wants them to make. What I find really helpful is where he says, when you take this offering, you are to set aside a sum of money in keeping with your income. That means, give to this offering in proportion with the money God has given you.

There are so many reasons this is helpful.

First, we see that God isn't comparing you to other people. He is looking at you and your personal situation and He understands what you are doing when you give.

Second, this also gives direction to people of every kind, young, old, poor, rich – everyone can find help in this. God isn't so much concerned with the amount you give, as He is that you be faithful in proportion to what He has given you.

When you give, don't worry if it doesn't seem like you are able to give as much as other people, just start by giving faithfully from what

God has given you. And, if from there you desire to give even more, you can do so, not out of fear or guilt; but, out of love and gratitude.

Today's Generosity Challenge:

Over dinner tonight open the conversation with this question: For our family what is the right percentage of giving in keeping with our income? But, before you respond, be prepared to justify your answer. What did you learn, how did their answer reflect their hearts and yours? Are you all aligned when it comes to giving? Or is there much to be done. Write down what you have observed here http://GenerousLife.net/Day28

Day 29 - Forgetting to please God

Hebrews 13:16

*[16] And do not forget to do good and to share with others,
for with such sacrifices God is pleased.*

Something all Christians are susceptible to is letting life distract us from what matters most. We are saved by this glorious Gospel, we are amazed by our God of love and grace, and then we just sort of fade out. We go to work, we pay bills, we cook meals, we go on errands and we lose sight of the big picture. We go from being passionately on fire for God to just going about ordinary life without much thought about our Father in heaven.

The author of Hebrews knew this about people, that when it comes down to it, we are the most forgetful sort of people. And he gave this reminder; "don't forget to do good and to share with others, for with such sacrifices God is pleased."

There are many reasons we don't do what pleases God. Sometimes we're stubborn, sometimes we don't know how, and, as the book of Hebrews mentions here, sometimes we just forget. When was the last time you made a point to do something good for or share with someone else?

Now let's go a step further, let's take out the ordinary sort of things like holding a door open or smiling at someone. When was the last time you did something good for someone and it meant you really had to go out of your way?

Now if you're like me, you might have trouble thinking of much you've done for others. And if you're like me, it's not that you didn't want to do good things, it's that you live a busy life and you just haven't gotten around to it yet.

So let's break the bad habit. Even today, go out and do something good for someone, share from what you have. And as you are doing so, know that you are pleasing God.

Today's Generosity Challenge:

This one is a little harder. Today, through prayer, pick up the phone and call someone you don't like, you know someone you're at odds with or their personality just bugs you – ask them out for coffee or lunch. Then, when you get together, ask them about themselves, say nothing about yourself. Just listen to understand, not to respond. And, when it's all over and you part ways just say, "Thank you for letting me know you a little better." (Be sure to pick up the check.) Then, go home and write down what you learned new about them here http://GenerousLife.net/Day29. Include how were you blessed.

Day 30 - Generous congregants

Galatians 6:6

⁶ Anyone who receives instruction in the word must share all good things with his instructor.

Most Americans today have very little trouble finding a church. There are churches everywhere: Big churches, small churches, contemporary churches, traditional churches. When someone moves, they hardly even need to think about a church because they'll just find one when they get to wherever they're going.

In a way, all these church choices are a huge blessing. I mean, what a blessing that we can hear the Bible preached all over the country. The downside, though, is that people sometimes stop thinking of their church as valuable. Rare things are valuable, common things aren't. If churches are common, then there is no perception of value. If the church I attend gets a little boring or stiff, or I just feel like a change, I can just leave – after all, there's another church just down the street. Sadly, that's how a lot of Christians treat their church.

But, Paul says in Galatians Chapter 6 that we need to share all good things with the people who give us instruction in the Word. This especially means our pastors. Our pastors labor in the Word for us. They pray for us. The Bible even tells us that God will call pastors to a high account for the job they do. Christians are called to show these pastors great generosity in all good things.

Do you pray for your pastor? Have you ever made him a meal? Do you share your God-given treasures with him? Do you, in general, live generously toward your pastor as the Bible tells you to?

Once you've been generous toward your pastor and church, you might also think about the different ministries that also bless you. Do you have a radio ministry or a magazine that regularly brings you blessing from the Word? Do you have friends or family who have been faithful to share with you from the Scriptures? If so, then you can be generous toward them, as well.

For all the ways people have encouraged you to live in God, you can encourage them right back with your generosity.

Today's Generosity Challenge:

This is simple. Before you head out the door today, call three folks, from your church or other Christian ministry, who have been instrumental in your spiritual growth. If it's an organization, ask to speak to the CEO or Pastor. Ask for a few minutes to tell them what they mean (or meant) to you. They'll be blessed and so will you. Make sure you journal the experience at http://GenerousLife.net/Day30. By the way, it's actually quite amazing how few people say "Thank you" to the ministers of the Gospel out there. So go ahead, make their day!

Day 31 - Generosity reveals what you value

Matthew 6:21
[21] For where your treasure is, there your heart will be also.

What do you treasure? It's important that we ask ourselves this question because it aids our decisions or discernment of how we want to live. For the person who treasures their career most of all, they will decide to make sacrifices in other parts of their life, perhaps in relation to relationships outside of work. For the person who treasures money or possessions, they might decide to sacrifice having a family, focusing on personal investment. For the person who treasures God's ways, you will see them willingly sacrifice worldly comforts like careers or pay raises as they discern what path God has for them in their life.

When Jesus talked about this in Matthew Chapter 6, he told us that we could build up treasure on earth, where thieves could take it and where moths and rust could destroy it, or we could build up treasure in heaven, where it would be eternally safe. And then he said this, "For where your treasure is, there your heart will be also."

So what's this have to do with generosity? Consider: If you highly treasure your money or possessions you are going to find it very hard to part with them in order to be generous to someone else. On the other hand, if you treasure God and the rewards He's promised in heaven above your earthly treasures, then you are going to realize it is totally worth it to give up your earthly treasure to gain heavenly treasure.

For us to be generous, we have to know what is valuable to us – and why. If you can't understand why you should want to be generous with others, it means that at some level you don't realize how much God has in store for you in heaven.

So, contemplate:
- God gave you His Son.
- Jesus gave you His life and His righteousness.
- Because of this, you have eternal blessing to look forward to.

Once that has taken root in your heart, being generous is all you'll want to be.

Today's Generosity Challenge:

Reflect on the last 30 days. What have you discovered about you own heart though this journey? Write down what you have seen about yourself here at http://GenerousLife.net/Day31.

Day 32 - You're more blessed to give than to receive

Acts 20:35
[35] *In everything I did, I showed you that by this kind of hard work we must help the weak, remembering the words the Lord Jesus himself said: 'It is more blessed to give than to receive.'*

Do you remember what Christmas morning felt like as a kid? Do you remember the excitement? Does the memory remind you of the suspense of wondering what might be under the Christmas tree for you? What amazing memories! All that joy, all that fun.

On the other hand, have you ever not known what to give someone? Have you ever shopped stressfully for someone with no idea if and how you will purchase anything they will like? Purchasing gifts is often difficult and stressful.

How funny it is, then, what Jesus said in Acts 20 – that it is more blessed to give than to receive. This might sound strange at first; after all, we've all experienced the enjoyable experience of receiving along with the stress of giving. But, Jesus isn't talking about what is easy or what is fun or anything like that. Jesus is talking about what God especially blesses. And God blesses both – but, giving more than receiving.

This verse is such an encouragement when we try to be generous. It is oftentimes a thankless job to be generous. Many might not notice your generosity. Some might feel entitled to your generosity. And some might go so far as to reject your generosity.

It can also be difficult on you to be generous. You have to ask yourself, "What am I willing to give up so that I can be generous?" And you might need to put aside something you would have loved, such as a vacation, an upgrade of some sort, an evening out with a loved one. That is why it is called sacrifice.

And let's pretend that things go totally awry and you do something really generous for someone who absolutely rejects it. You know what? God's word is still true and your giving is still blessed.

Whatever response to your generosity, good, bad, or somewhere in between, God is pleased with your giving and he will bless it. Receiving things might be fun; but, giving is blessed.

Today's Generosity Challenge:

Again, reflect on the blessing you have received in this generosity journey. Now, through prayer, thank the Lord for the blessings you have received. Be sure to write them down here at http://GenerousLife. net/Day32.

Day 33 - Gospel-motivated generosity

Exodus 35:21

21 and everyone who was willing and whose heart moved him came and brought an offering to the LORD for the work on the Tent of Meeting, for all its service, and for the sacred garments.

"So what?"

Most often, this is the response of a teenager with some attitude. You tell them something and they respond, "So what?" Or in other words, how does that matter to me? I think this is a useful question for us to ask ourselves, especially when it comes to the things that we hold as most important in our lives. I don't have any illusions that it's a useful question from an upset teenager's mouth; but, if we ask it seriously of ourselves, especially in regard to our faith, we can really be blessed.

Exodus, Chapter 35, describes how the people of God were gathering resources to work on the tent of meeting. The people who gave to the work were described as those who were willing and whose heart moved them to give. These people didn't just say, "Wow this is a great cause, good luck." Rather, because they valued the cause, they allowed the motivation of their hearts to spur them on to give generously.

I think we can really learn from their example.

Believers today have an amazing gospel of grace. The Son of God, Himself, came to earth, died on a cross, rose from the grave and earned eternal life for His people in the process. Isn't this is incredible Good News we have?! And if you're a believer, I hope you're agreeing with me right now. I hope your heart over flows when you hear this Good News proclaimed.

But, this is where we make sure this is personal. You are a child of God, bought by the blood of Jesus. How does that affect how you live?

In other words, "so what?"

If the Gospel has saved you, if it motivates you, if it excites you, then, like the believers of old, let the generosity of your life express the passion of your heart.

Today's Generosity Challenge:

As you go about your day today, think of all the people with whom you will come into contact – your co-workers, the bank teller, your family. Make a little plan about how to express the love and generosity of Jesus to them. Maybe it's a kind word or an expression of gratitude, a time of prayer, maybe a little gift or thoughtful card: Just a simple expression of love. Just do it for at least one day. Write down how your observations here http://GenerousLife.net/Day33. Then make another plan for tomorrow.

Day 34 - Learn to Revere God

Deuteronomy 14:22-23
²² Be sure to set aside a tenth of all that
your fields produce each year.
²³ Eat the tithe of your grain, new wine and oil, and the firstborn
of your herds and flocks in the presence of the LORD
your God at the place He will choose as a dwelling for His Name,
so that you may learn to revere the LORD your God always.

One of the things mature Christians learn over the course of their lives is how to honor God in practical ways. You see it's one thing to just say, "I love God," or "I worship God," or things similar to that. But, let's admit it, its not always clear or easy as to how we show that with our lives. Talking the talk of Christianity is one thing, walking the walk is another. So what can we do to show with our lives how we feel toward God?

In the Old Testament, God gives us something helpful for this. In Deuteronomy, Chapter 14, God gives some very detailed instructions on giving. If we read through too fast, we'd think this was just like the IRS tax code for ancient Israel. But, when you stop to read it, you see that God says that all these instructions are so that they can learn to revere the Lord their God always. God is teaching us here that giving is a tangible way that we show honor and devotion to God.

In our lives, we are tempted to think that our generosity is just about the ministry or cause or people we give to. We can also be tempted to think our generosity has nothing to do with our faith in God. But, God helps us to lift our eyes heavenward when we give.

Giving to God's causes – like your church or a God-honoring ministry that blesses you – is you parting with your earthly treasure so that God's will would be done. In so doing, you are saying, "God, your will is more important than my treasure – and it is really Your treasure that You have given me to manage for You, anyway." As you pursue your generous life, you also are learning day by day to revere God.

Today's Generosity Challenge:

Reflect today on how you have learned to revere God though this journey of generosity. Write down what you have learned about the character of God through this journey here at http://GenerousLife.net/ Day34.

Day 35 - Generosity is part of the whole package

Matthew 23:23
[23] *"Woe to you, teachers of the law and Pharisees, you hypocrites! You give a tenth of your spices – mint, dill, and cumin. But, you have neglected the more important matters of the law – justice, mercy, and faithfulness. You should have practiced the latter, without neglecting the former.*

Sometimes I do the right thing; but I'll do it for the wrong reason. Can you relate to that?

You know, I'll do something like say 'please' and 'thank you;' but only to get something for myself. Or in a bigger way, I'll go to church to fellowship with other believers and not be thinking about how I'm there to worship God. It's not that having either good manners or fellowship is bad. The problem arises when I neglect the more important things when I do them.

Our generosity can be similar to this, too. Sometimes when we are trying to be generous toward God or toward our neighbor, our generosity is completely external. Outside we might be smiling and helping; but, inside we are hard-hearted and resenting the generosity we are showing.

In Matthew, Chapter 23, Jesus called out people in His time that did something similar. He criticized religious leaders who were fervently – and legalistically – hooked on giving. They even gave from the herbs and spices they grew in their gardens! But, you know where these people went wrong? They neglected more important things like justice, mercy, and faithfulness. Jesus goes on to say that they should have been giving without neglecting the more important things of their faith.

Likewise, when you are being generous, God cares about the heart you bring to your generosity. Your generosity goes hand-in-hand with your love for God and neighbor, your desire to bear a good testimony for God and your desire that God always be glorified in what you do. Generosity is a central characteristic of Christians; but, it is not the only trait and God would never have you sacrifice something more important so that you could appear to be living generously.

Today's Generosity Challenge:

Be honest, when in the last 34 days have you just gone through the motions in your generosity? Maybe your heart was completely wrong? Maybe you just didn't care? Through prayer ask the Lord, WHY? Then write down your answers here at http://GenerousLife.net/Day35

Day 36 - Honoring with God with what is valuable

Malachi 1:7-8

[7] "You place defiled food on my altar. "But, you ask, 'How have we defiled you?' "By saying that the LORD's table is contemptible. [8] When you bring blind animals for sacrifice, is that not wrong? When you sacrifice crippled or diseased animals, is that not wrong? Try offering them to your governor! Would he be pleased with you? Would he accept you?" says the LORD Almighty.

Do you ever find you sometimes treat the people you care most about worse than you treat people you barely know? For example, some people spend all day at work. They're helping customers and clients; they're taking orders from the boss. And all day long they do a great job, with patience and kindness. But, then they return home to their family and they just don't have anything left over after the day. So the family gets the irritation, or the short responses, or what you will.

When I've been guilty of this I look at myself and think, "What are you doing? How are you going to treat everyone in the world as good as you can and then go and just give the leftovers to the ones you love the most? I think many of us can relate to doing this kind of thing. Unfortunately, people have acting this way toward God for a long time.

In Malachi, Chapter 1, God really goes after that attitude. He tells his people they've been defiling his altar. When they were supposed to bring the best of their flocks for their offerings, they were bringing blind, crippled, and diseased animals.

And God was not pleased at all about it.

And God makes a great point; He says you wouldn't give offerings like that to your governors, so how are you going to go and give me, your God and redeemer, these offerings that mean so little to you?

We can really see ourselves in these people, can't we?

We're reminded that God deserves our absolute best. Not the things we don't care about, not the things where it doesn't matter one way or the other if we do, which are basically our leftovers. Don't let your generosity toward God be tainted by a desire to give as little as possible.

God gave us His own Son. Let us, then, give Him what is precious in our eyes, as well.

Today's Generosity Challenge:

Think about those you love most. Do they get your generous best? If not, why not? Now, with a repentant heart go to each of them about what the Lord has shown you and make your confession. Ask them for their help in repentance. Write down you experience here at http://GenerousLife.net/Day36.

Day 37 - Rejoicing in generosity

1 Chronicles 29:9
*⁹ The people rejoiced at the willing response of their leaders,
for they had given freely and wholeheartedly to the LORD.
David, the king, also rejoiced greatly.*

When we were young believers, most of us needed some guidance. God saved us and then we had to figure out what came next. It's precisely at this moment of time that I treasure the people who encouraged me in what was right. Telling me to sit down and regularly read the Word, pray to God, seek fellowship with other believers. Vital acts. If it weren't for this kind of godly encouragement I don't know where I would be.

As believers, we need this kind of encouragement in relation to our generosity as well. In 1 Chronicles, Chapter 29, the people are called to give to the work of building the temple. The people gave generously and the Scriptures record that "the people rejoiced at the willing response of their leaders, for they had given freely and wholeheartedly to the LORD." The people might have resisted, lamenting all the treasure that was given to this project. But, believing in the cause, they rejoiced to see their leaders responding so generously. To some extent, it must also have been encouraging to the leaders. They were responding generously in faith, giving from the treasure with which they were entrusted. There surely was potential for fear of man to creep in and prevent them from their generosity. But, they used their leadership to honor God generously and the people rejoiced.

We, too, have this same ability to influence and encourage generosity in others. Toward our church leaders, we can encourage them for the commitment they have made in being generous. We can support them when they have made important sacrifices in that generosity to God. In our relationships of any kind, let us be as quick to encourage someone in their generosity as we would their humility or knowledge of the Word.

Generosity does not only involve the person who is willing to give. It also depends upon those who are committed to encouraging them.

Today's Generosity Challenge:

From whom have you seen real generosity demonstrated? How can you celebrate it, thank them, or help them with the burden? Put this into action. And help by praising their generosity and standing by them! Be sure to write it down here at http://GenerousLife.net/Day37

Day 38 - The privilege of generosity

2 Corinthians 8:3-4

3 For I testify that they gave as much as they were able, and even beyond their ability. Entirely on their own,
4 they urgently pleaded with us for the privilege of sharing in this service to the saints.

We have an understandably human reaction when we do something generous for someone else: we expect to be thanked. After all, we just went out of our way to do something above and beyond, and it's just the natural thing to do that they would thank us. But, you know what? When we're generous with others, we should be grateful, too.

A great example of this is in 2 Corinthians, Chapter 8. There, Paul describes just how passionately the Macedonian churches wanted to help. He says that even though they were living in extreme poverty and trial, their joy for the Lord welled up, reflected in rich generosity. They even went so far that they were pleading with Paul to be given the privilege (the privilege!) of sharing in the service to the saints.

I find their example so humbling. Here these people are, barely getting by on their own. Yet despite their circumstances and because of the joy of the Gospel, they are chomping at the bit to be generous with others. And I can think of so many examples in my own life when, even though I was living way more comfortably than these Macedonian churches probably were, I dodged opportunities to give to ministries or missionaries. And sometimes when I did give I didn't do it with a joyful heart.

My prayer for my own life – and for yours – is that we would have the perspective of the Macedonian believers. The truth is that it is our immense privilege to be children of God and, not only that, he goes on to use our small lives and our generosity to work out his plans in the world. So the next time you do something generous for someone, they may or may not thank you. But, if these Macedonians inspire you the way they inspire me, you might just thank them.

<u>Today's Generosity Challenge:</u>

Who are the "Macedonians" in your life that need to be thanked? Write them down and why here at http://GenerousLife.net/Day38. Then pick up the phone to them and say, "Thank you!"

Day 39 - Excellent Giving

2 Corinthians 8:7
⁷ But, just as you excel in everything – in faith, in speech,
in knowledge, in complete earnestness and in
your love for us – see that you also excel in this grace of giving.

If we were asked what we would like to improve in our Christian walk, we would likely say things like knowing the Word better, loving our neighbor, being more faithful in our lives, knowing how to talk about our faith more effectively, etc. But, the word of God adds one that might not be as high on the list in our minds: God wants us to grow in our generosity.

In Paul's second letter to the Corinthians Chapter 8, he encourages them to excel. He says you excel in faith, in speech, in knowledge, in complete earnestness and in your love. These are all huge things, aren't they? Then, he adds this: "See that you also excel in this grace of giving." He says, right along with all these big Christian virtues like love, faith and knowledge that we need to be pursuing this grace of giving. And that's not just pursuing on the side; but excelling.

What do you think of when you think of someone excelling? For me, I think of people like the athletes in the Olympics. Those people excel. They spend more time training in one month than I do in a year. They have dedicated their lives to their sport. And when they get to that stage in the Olympics, they have proven themselves to be among the very best in the world.

In a way far more important than an Olympic event, God has stated for each of us to excel in our generosity. In whatever ways we have been gifted to be generous, whether with our time, our talents, or our treasure, God wants excellence in how we give those away. Don't be mistaken; God doesn't love you better because you give generously. But, because God has loved us so much, we can now go forth and live generously.

Today's Generosity Challenge:

How have you been inspired to live more generously? What are you plans? Write them down at http://GenerousLife.net/Day39

Day 40 - Sending the Good News

Romans 10: 14-15

*[14] How, then, can they call on the one they have not believed in?
And how can they believe in the one of whom they have not heard?
And how can they hear without someone preaching to them?
[15] And how can they preach unless they are sent? As it is written,
"How beautiful are the feet of those who bring good news!"*

You know one thing I always notice about shows like the Academy Awards? It's all the people the winners thank. You know, winner of best actress gets up there and says I want to thank all these people, and they get out a piece of paper with long list of names on it. They're thanking their friends, their family, the director, the fellow actors, the nanny, everyone who was involved in their success. I think it's really interesting how many people are involved in just one person's success.

The spread of the Gospel is really very similar. Paul, in Romans, Chapter 10, talks about how important it is that people have the Gospel preached to them. He says, "People aren't going to be saved unless someone tells them about Jesus..." A second point he makes is this; no one is going to be able to hear the Gospel unless we send people out. This all seems to make sense; but we don't always realize how important a role the everyday person (you and me) has to play in this.

See, we think the only people spreading the Gospel are the missionaries or the pastors or some other prominent Christian figure. And I absolutely praise God for these people. But, just like the actor winning the award, those pastors, missionaries, or whoever didn't get there on their own. The Gospel doesn't get sent out unless people generously support it. It's so important for people to realize that their support of Gospel work is absolutely essential in the work of the Kingdom. When you are willing to be generous in participating with God in His work, no matter its form, you play an important role. You may not be the one preaching; but, in the spread of God's gospel, your generosity plays an indispensable role.

Today's Generosity Challenge:

Do you know that only about two percent of all Christians have ever shared the Gospel with another person! How can we love our generous Lord without telling others? Are we not enthusiastic, thankful and over-joyed? Your task today is to find one person and share Christ with them, verbally, intentionally and in love. Now, write down their response here at http://GenerousLife.net/Day40.

Day 41 - Walking the Walk

James 2:18
[18] *But, someone will say, "You have faith; I have deeds." Show me your faith without deeds, and I will show you my faith by what I do.*

You can talk the talk; but can you walk the walk?

That's the leadership literature buzz-phrase for it, anyway.

In our lives, it is a lot easier to talk about amazing things than it is to live those things daily.

The Bible knows what a struggle it can be to synchronize our beliefs and our actions. And I don't want you to think I'm saying that it's supposed to be easy, because Scripture doesn't say that at all. But, one thing the Bible does say is this, how we live out our beliefs is important.

When James writes his letter, in the second chapter, he describes two people having a sort of hypothetical show down. One says, "I have faith;" but, he has no action to show it. So the second person responds, "I won't just tell you I have faith, I also have actions that prove my faith."

Actually, our lives really do play out our real beliefs. What we realize here; however, is how important it is that our life agrees with the beliefs we, as Christians, profess.

This works out in every aspect of our life. But, here, let's just take generosity, for example.

We can talk all day about how God wants us to be generous and how we are supposed to live generously because God has been so generous to us in the Gospel.

But, then – what?

And so, then – what do we do?

Today's Generosity Challenge:
As this is the last day in our journey together, I'd encourage you to try something new. Get out a pen and paper. Jot down how you feel you personally should show generosity in your life from here forward. Don't

think you have to bring about world peace; but, just pick some way or ways that you can be generous each day. Then, go do them. And as you do so, pray that the world sees that by God's grace, you also walk the walk. Make your moving forward pledge here at http://GenerousLife. net/Day41

Take the Ultimate Generosity Challenge

Rarely does your generosity motivate others into their own personal lifestyle of generosity. But we want to challenge you to encourage others in their generosity and take the ultimate challenge. You've seen how the Holy Spirit will deeply change you with daily generosity challenges.

Now, take the ultimate generosity challenge and buy one book for your friends and your pastor. Ask them to read it and take the daily challenge. Imagine what might just happen next.

Order additional copies at www.AJourneyToGenerosity.com
Or call 877-383-5831

CPSIA information can be obtained
at www.ICGtesting.com
Printed in the USA
LVHW101742260723
753091LV00003B/383